TO WHOEVER HE HAS BECOME

Anu Nicholas

ISBN: 9798338076293

Minute man

Timer

He is lost

And he believes that he has no one

A man who has no cure for his loneliness

None found in this world

All love that comes around him perishes

A love that his heart wants but cannot be found

Struggled Man

A man without company

Loneliness is his companion

Surrounded by it

A friend who does not speak

But its silence is deafening

He is a man who struggles

A man destined to struggle on the earth

Searching but not finding

Talking but not being listened to

Always met with silence

Always building but in the same way

Destroying what he has built

A man who wanders on his own

Talkative Pavilion

A man who wanders with his words

He is a man who will always be forgotten

He would be recognised for his lies

The way he charms with words

But not recognised as being honest

He is a man who has a way with words

But a man who fails at them

A man who will long and will search

And he will never find

Stuck in time and in his valley of lies

Calling Time

He calls and calls because he is lonely

Searching for someone to connect

But always his calls will always be declined

The man who wants to talk

But always falls in the trap of being behind the phone

Shell of the sand

A man who talks for hours

But a man who is not listened to

A man who appears to be sane

But his mind often wanders and suffers

A man who is close to giving up

And he believes that he has been forgotten

A man who is stuck in his mind for hours

The one who's hiding

To the man who is hiding his affections

To the man who has to wait

To the man who is searching and longing

To the man who hides his feelings

To the man who hides all of himself

The Familiar

Doubting himself felt more familiar

Then taking care of himself and loving himself

Rejection felt much more familiar

Then looking after himself

Denying himself of everything good

Sadness has always been familiar in his life

Loving

He was always told that he loved too much
He was too extreme with his affection
Much too touchy
And much too friendly
His love was infectious, but it had no love brought to him
All that love but he did not receive it

9

Four corridors

A man who hides within the four corridors of his heart

Searching but never finding

Seeking but never wishing to be found

Wanting but never accepting the want

A man who hides in the four corridors of his mind

The Loneliest Man

Trapped in being alone

He will be the one who is forgotten

Not because of his loneliness

But because of seclusion

Choosing to be away from anyone who does not appeal to their

eyes

Wanting and waiting for a prize

Instead of loving himself

Desiring for others

But never looking inside and changing

He is the loneliest man ever

Minute Man

One minute he is lonely

One minute he is tired

One minute he wants love

The next he declines it

One minute he is searching for a partner

The next he is put off by the lover

He is a man who is living in minutes

As the time ticks

He is stuck, not wanting to wander

Trapped in being alone

Never wanted

He is never wanted by the right person
Though he desires it
He is never pleased by the outcome of the person
Though when the right person appears he shuns it
He is a man whose mind is transfixed in finding his other
But a man who is stuck in his ways
So much so that he finds himself crying and saying
"I am never wanted."

The Hollow

A man who truly feels forgotten

A man who wanders and feels like he cannot speak

A man who tries to reach out

But still feels forgotten

A man who searches but his heart is dismissed

Time Wanderer

A man who struggles only loses when he has completely given up
And when he has forgotten of those who long for his affection
A man who allows time to wither him away
He will always be the man who loses everything
A man who uses money to cement his sorrow
He will always see his successes topple
For money comes
And money goes

Time waits for no man

Time waits for no one

Just as a send-off to his formal self

Time waits for no man

Not even the loneliest

A man who was stuck behind a desk

A man who is stuck behind the screen

A man who longs for a love that is not seen

A man who is trapped behind hours and minutes

The Lost Boy

The past made him feel like a little boy
The smallest boy without a father
A boy who looked to women for help
But was met with frustration and crying
A young boy who was brought to become a man
Ripped away from his innocence
Hard emotions
And an even hardened heart
A man who became a figurine
Bounds of pride from his mother in his later years
But his actions bound a price
Costing his mind
Years later feeling exhausted and humiliated
Not being able to find his other rib
And other causes of sin
In his saddest moments
When he could not cry out to daddy
And he could not stress out his mother
That little boy appeared again
The lost and hopeless boy

Hopeless Dream

Seconds dragged out in days

The best moments were around his friends

The worst moments were when he was home alone in his bed

A mind that was filled with dark thoughts and feelings

Exhausted with problems and tribulations

Hands that fiddled with anxiety

A man lost with no world to wander

Unveiling Man

Instead of uncovering his feelings

He bottled it up

Enough wraps could cover even the worst up

Just a few more pieces

Just more hidden objects

Just enough to make the gift so bulky

It would become unrecognisable

Feelings trapped because they were a curse to him

Bound in lies

And stashed in sin

Lonely Road

Before he walked on the loneliest road
Asking for help but never finding it
Searching but never getting
But Jesus Christ showed up
When the only person reached out to him
Like a blinding light in a sea of darkness
It echoed into his heart
Changing him
Making his lonely road
Filled with brothers and sisters in Christ
He could give up his lonely life
To join in the presence of the Father and his Son Jesus Christ

A man trapped by the shadows

A man who would not listen

Indulging what was not good for his so

Until it took away all the light his mother had sown

Each woman and friend took his light

Piece by piece removing his light

Until he became an even darkened shadow

The man inside

He is a harsh man

Words never came out properly

A man trapped by the deepest secrets in his life

Grown-up by women

Forced to be objectified by horrible friends

Until it became his personality

A man who grew up in darkness

Until the darkness is what he grew used to

Glass

Trapped in poor habits and lifestyle
His heart grew cold
It started slowly, like a cold breeze
Then the air became misty
The grass of his past crept up
Until it froze over and was forgotten
When it came close to his heart
He completely turned away from his pain
Too painful to stare at it for too long
Instead, he rather let his heart stay chilled instead

Fields

It would take him many lives to remove the sins of his past

Many other moments

The time someone had ruined his life

Even for a glimpse of a moment

Instead of making peace

He broke others

And blaming others for his hurt and humiliation

Instead of accepting his moment of shame

He would rather hide in the valley

Then, he waters his own garden

Souls

Dark souls of the past
They always found a way of coming back
Until one soul came with the light
The glimmer of light which almost made him cower to the
darkness
A light that was unrecognisable in the darkness
A light that stuck in his mind
A light that kept him up at work
A light that held unto him on the darkest days
Especially at night when he cried to himself
It was a soul that was redeemed from all darkness

Hidden

Those who stay hidden will always be found

Though in the darkness

Those who wish can hide

But it is in the light

Darkness will be eradicated

Glimpse

It dulled his senses when he found the light

It stuck beside him

A drink could not hold him

Fancy words could not damage him into ruin his soul

Not even shiny objects

He saw a glimpse of the light

And he could not pull away

By seeing a glimpse of light

He was able to see the renewing of his soul

Broken tower

At the night

It was always a fight

Whether from his mind or his body

Darkness was uncomfortable then

He was able to see himself without a mirror

A little person

A man who held to the intangible wealth

A man who would instantly break after experiencing rejection

A man who was fearful of himself

Curtain

A curtain was always shown

A person who was loved but only partially

His heart was too switched off to accept love

He had hidden the person he was behind a curtain

Heavenly

It wasn't love that he recognised

Many people said that they loved him, but they were always wrong

There was always someone better

Someone more good-looking

Someone who out-performed more in the relationship

But he had not recognised the beauty God had given him

He had not recognised the gifts and talents bestowed on him

He was filled with empty cups who enjoyed taking from others

That is why he could never fit in

His cup needed to be overflowed

And it could not be done by others

It had to be done by Him

Heartbroken

Surrounded by pain he was left with a painful decision
To live in shame or survive just a while longer
One more
Just one more object to keep him alive
But with every decision
He was left deeper and deeper away from God
In the hands of the darkness
And as a prize for the enemy
Instead of cleaning his soul
He allowed the darkness to have a hold on him
His heart did not break because of past relationships
It was broken because with every decision he never chose himself
He always chose the darkness

Jesus Loves You

It took him a while to accept that someone had loved him

Despite all of the bad he had done

His heart was filled with longing and shame

Longing for love

But ashamed by how far he went for it

The Son of God was always there for him

Instead, he looked at people

Unfilled cups to keep him watered

The three words that softened his cold heart were

Jesus Loves You

Filled by Him

The Holy Spirit filled him when he knew of Jesus

He gave his heart

Cold and ashamed

A heart of stone

That had been soften by Jesus Christ

Loving II

As his faith grew
The love he gave was not squandered
The love that he felt was not wasted
For the Son of God had loved him
His love was cherished
And brought back
The love he gave was finally found
Because he experienced a perfect love
Jesus Christ

Hope and Refuge

The Lord charged him

When he was lost and needed hope

He carried him through

All his pain and anxiety

All his suffering and anger

Being his hope and refuge from the hurt and pain

Companionship

Jesus has a companionship which was unknown

To him in his life

He changed his life and restored him

Allowing him to be healed

So, he could accept the friendships around him

Providing a light and love that comes from Jesus Christ

Safe Place

Jesus is the safe place

The change where the truth can come out without judgment or
punishment

A chance to repent

And become new

Losing a life to gain a life

A life so pure

Not moved

He was not moved

Jesus stuck beside him

A rock that he could stand by

Firm and strong

He built his foundation on the rock

As the sand of sin washed away

His new identity grew stronger

Under his Pavilion

He was in his care

He was finally free

Pass judgement and hate

He was in a state of peace which could only happen

By the Grace and power of the Lord

Under his care he was safe

He is loved

He is cared for

He is looked after

Just like everyone else

And the Father and Son waits for others to join them

His Heart

Jesus Christ had taken his heart

Talking to him

And knowing him

Restoring hope and peace within him

Restoring who he should be

Purifying his soul

Restoring him to who he is

Not reminding him of who he was

He captured his heart

And in doing so his love overflows

Letting Go

He could finally let go of the past

Letting goes of the pain that was truly in him

Letting goes of those who had hurt him

And fixing the relationships of those he had hurt

Why?

Because the Father had soothed him

And the Son of God restored him

He was overcome by love

So much so that he finally had peace

Finding peace in letting go

Peace with Him

The peace from Jesus Christ overflowed

And it came to the centre

Coming close to his heart

He was no longer bound in shackles of the past

Jesus had freed him

And freedom from Jesus is sweet

Gratitude

He was fond of Jesus

Not because of what he had done

But because of his indescribable love

Despite his past, Jesus loved him

No one could cast the first stone

He had freedom and peace by knowing that Jesus Christ loved

him

And for that he was grateful

He was grateful that despite his past

Now he would have finally found happiness

A happiness not bound by time or by bad decisions

A love and happiness coming from the sacrifice of Jesus Christ on

the cross

And for that penalty

He will live in freedom forevermore

Sings of Him

The Lord sings over him

Day after day

Never leaving him

Or forgetting about him

He longed for him

Hoping that one day he would search for him

So that he would be seen one day

By the Father himself

Through the help of Jesus Christ

Smile

He could finally smile

No longer trapped in sin and shame

His smiles would come straight from the heart

Where Jesus lives

Smiles could bear no deceit behind it

It was true

It was real

A smile filled light

Changes and Lead

Jesus freed him from the sins of his past

He has his freedom in Christ

Changed and in love

Not bounded by the past

But freed through the blood of Jesus Christ

Because he changed

He let Jesus lead him

Living in the truth was so much sweeter than living in sin

Trust in Him

He was able to trust him

Because he loved him so much

Jesus took a chance on him

When everyone else left him

Jesus always stayed beside him

He encouraged him

And when all else

When things became hard

Jesus always came in the end

A saviour to the hopeless

A friend to those who love

A saviour of the whole world

Close to him

Jesus was close to him

Being beside him during his darkest days

Helping him when he was struggling

Keeping by him

When he grew quiet and wanted to give up

The Lord helped him

The goodness of Him is what touched his heart and changed him

Praise the Lord!

Led Through Fire

He led him through the pain and the heart

And restored the fire in his heart

Helping him after he surrendered his chaotic life to him

Jesus Christ fixed him

By making him known that his sin was not him

By sin he was born in

But by Jesus he was redeemed

Indescribable Love

Love from God was indescribable like a current of emotions

A love where a father could completely love him and cherish him

A man who was seeking a love that could not be seen

A love that his heart and soul will cherish always

A love that moves so deeply and powerfully

A love from the Greatest Father

Dear Father God

A Father who is filled with Grace which is unending

A father who lives a life that we all can all attest to

A father who looks after his son

A father who cares for the uncared

And helps to the helpless

Helpful to the creation

And good to the helpless

A keeper in a time of trouble

A promise in a time of crisis

A God with we can call out to and he will still answer

A God who stands firm in the time of trouble

Jacob's promise

Father I will not go

I will not flee until I am blessed

Place your blessings on me

So that I may become free in the spirit

So, my soul can have the reason to fight again

So, my mind can feel light again

Father, please help your dear son in time of trouble

Help me, Lord!

Hear my cry!

I will not go until I am blessed!

And have a life that I can attest

Matthew 11:28

Three wise men humbled themselves

Coming close to the Father through the son

Giving Him gifts to come

Placing themselves away from the world

And having a touch of the world

The Father is close to those who are weary

He helps the lonely wanderer

He calms them in still waters

He restores our soul

Jesus Christ

He is the hope to the hopeless

He is the love of the unlovable

He is the God that all are searching for

He is Jesus Christ

King of the universe

Alongside the maker of the whole world

He is a touch of peace

Freedom from wicked ways

A bouquet of hope in the plainest fields

Jesus is the truth, the light and the way

My Jesus, My Saviour

Jesus has taken the thorn out of his heart

And made it a heart of gold

By accepting him and loving him

Within a second of surrendering he felt God's presence in his life

Praise the Lord

His Side

Returning to Jesus was hard

But living in a world of sin was harder

Harder to control

Harder to love himself through Jesus's eyes

Harder to better himself

Being by Jesus' side meant he was looked after

Loved and cherished

He will never leave his side

His Light

Memories of the path used to have him stuck

In sin and shame

But being with Jesus

He has been renewed

And not blamed

Through repentance

And giving his life to Christ

He has received a new hope, a clearer life

A life filled with purpose

And hope

In Your Presence

The nature of God has shaken his life

The past he longed for had disappeared

He found strength in loving him

He found hope in knowing him

He found love in his presence

The Father's presence is good

God is a good God

Rebuild

Jesus rebuilt everything in his life

When he wanted to give up

And was always on the edge

Jesus helped him

He built him up

Loving him

Sacrificing his shame and his past

So that he can be healed and happy

Jesus rebuilt his life

So that over every building

There was the light that was always shining over it

Peace in You

Peace is found in Jesus Christ

The peace of love

The peace longing for in the mind

The peace that is above all understanding

A peace that is restored and can be achieved in Jesus Christ

Serve Him

And find peace within Him

In Your Presence

In God's presence
He felt the power of God
The life that he led before did not taste the same
The power of His Son Jesus Christ
It changed his life
By visiting their presence
Knowing how sweet his love is
By knowing Jesus's presence and love towards him
He learned to love himself

No more shame

Hurt and shame were removed

Because he cried

He called for him and received help

Jesus is Faithful

He removed all shame and regret

This young man's heart was changed

So, in adulthood, he would serve him with his heart filled with
gladness

Jesus's Presence

Jesus's presence is sweet and certain

Showing his goodness and truth

Jesus is a helper in a time of trouble

He never blocks obstacles but removes them

He hears the cries

And he answers

Restoring the mind and the soul

Jesus's presence is holy and powerful

When his name is mentioned

Demons scatter

It is because Jesus Christ lives!

Loved by Him

Jesus was the first to truly love him

Those who loved him often sabotaged their relationship with him

Growing up he had to deny himself love

Lost wandering what was bad

He concluded that it was him

But Jesus was the first to love

To change his heart

And realise that it is by Grace he is saved

That the bad was not him

But he was truly loved

Laid Down

He laid down his shame

He laid down his pain and anxiety

He helped him when he struggled to sleep

Jesus laid down everything

The sins of his life

By dying on the cross

He changed him and restored him

The power of Jesus Christ is living hope

Hope in a living form

For His Grace, he is saved

For his lost hope

He has saved him and restored

He laid everything down on the line

From the little boy to the adult who longed for love

Never Change

Jesus Christ never changed

He was enough for him

As his unsatisfied soul wrestled for something more

Jesus was enough

Because he never changed

He gave him the life he so desperately longed for

Changing him and growing him into a better man

Because he never changed

He as a man was restored

Praise the Lord! For he is good, and his mercies endure forever!

Faithful Jesus

Jesus is faithful

Always waiting until the door is knocked

Waiting when he felt like he could not get up

Waiting when he searched for live-in people

Who did not love him back

Knowing Jesus now

Knowing the faithfulness of Jesus Christ

He too would have faith in Him

Loving Child

Jesus loved him so much

That the child in him felt loved

He felt changed and loved

The peace in him was restored

Jesus is always good and loving

Taking hold of his life

And giving him a better life

A life he can be proud of

Jesus is the same

Jesus does not change like men

His heart is not pushed and filled with darkness

He stays the same

Though the sin and the neglect

Jesus never changes

A loving and helpful guide in a time of trouble

The King that surpasses all knowledge on earth

Removing shame and pride from us all

Restoring hope in communities

And love in hearts

Praise ye the Lord!

For He is the same and he never changes!

Faith Renewed

Jesus renews faith in all

Providing clarity and light in life

Changing the hearts of man

So that they will be restored and given life again

Faith is renewed during every trial

And helped before the defeat

Jesus Christ is the same Jesus who restored healing to the woman

who touched his hem

He will restore and give hope to all

Restoring and acknowledging faith

Rewarded

In the past, he believed that the reward was love

To seek for love in all of the darkest places to be rewarded for it

But Jesus showed that this was not the case

The reward was seeking Jesus Christ in all things

Placing his life for Jesus Christ

Asking for help to Him during his good times and his times of crisis

Jesus restored his soul

Helping him along the way

The reward was not love

The reward was gaining a new life in Jesus Christ

Love was a product of that reward

Praise the Lord!

For he is good and works wonders in our lives!

Peace

Jesus is the peace his soul craved
The peace that removes all pain and evil
Restoring the soul to the place it needs to be
Peace that was further than all acknowledgement
A peace that restored those around him
Peace that came from God
Through Jesus Christ

Friend

The Father is a friend to all who are righteous

Men and women who go out of their way to serve him

He gained three friends on his journey

A love from God

The presence of Jesus Christ

And a friend in the Holy Spirit

So, his talents can be used for God

And to show the goodness of God

Throne

Jesus took place in his heart

Taking the throne and conquering the darkness

So that darkness will not have a place in his life again

He can now serve with gladness and hope

That his Father had sent his son to help him

The Throne of God is known

And is waiting for him

The seasons of sadness will be turned into a season of Joy

The King is on his throne

Parts of Him

The parts of him

That needed love

The heart that longed for love

The body that was tired and exhausted from work

The man who became a child whenever rejection appeared

The Jesus was there and close to him

Though he thought otherwise

He helped his heart

Healed his heart

So, he could serve him with sincerity

Changing my Heart

The Lord changes the weakest hearts

Healing them and making them pure

Those who have been unsatisfied with life

He restores and heals

Praise the Lord!

Moved

The Lord moved his heart

Removing the anxiety from him

Restoring his mentality

So that he can become a better person to Him

God is close to those who are heartbroken

Jesus restores those who have been captured by sin

The Lord Heals

The Father Heals

Praise be their Name!

The Soother

The Lord has shaped me and built me
He has placed me firmly in his pavilion
Pouring honey and oil into my life
Blessing me so that I can be changed
The Lord blesses those who seek Him
He heals those who call Him
He has restored my soul
Praise ye the Lord!

Trust in His Guidance

He could trust in God's guidance

Because he had walked alongside Jesus Christ

Jesus was with him during his darkest days

He was there beside him

He loved him and took care of him

Jesus restored him

He trusted in his guide

Because in his guidance Jesus always showed goodness

I receive

He believed in Jesus Christ

He believed in his promises

Because he felt different

The love he wanted and search for

It was always there

He received Jesus Christ in his heart

Because Jesus Christ was the only person that could help him

By Faith

The smallest faith restored his life

Faith is as small as a mustard seed

It is by Faith he has been restored

It is by Faith his life is renewed

It is by Faith he does not need to walk in shame

It is by Faith Jesus Christ rose again

I Walk

I walk in Faith knowing that Jesus Christ has saved me

He has taken away my sin

And he has made me whole

Everything else is based on Him

He is my conqueror

And he is my provider

Praise the Lord

Yours to Lead

Jesus led him

Through the fires deep in his heart

Through the darkest fields

Leading him to a place where he could rest

Then being able to be restored and brought to peace

Jesus Christ understood him

And therefore, he would follow Jesus Christ's lead

He will lead his life for now and forever

Love From Him

Not Afraid

He is not afraid of the past or his future

Because the capturer of the past has healed him

He has removed all shame

And provided hope

In His name

Jesus Christ

In You I am Safe

Learning to love Him was easy

Because Jesus Christ made it easy

It was easy to accept the Grace sent by God

Because Jesus made it easy

It was not a lie he told himself

Jesus is his safe place

Because Jesus Christ chose him first

Safe Forever

He is safe forever
Because he knows him
He has met the King of the God
Who walked amongst us
A king who is fair and just
A king who loves all of us
A king who lives forever
King Jesus!

Trusting

He couldn't trust himself, but he could trust Jesus Christ

He is his light and his hope

A friend in a time of trouble

A love that just can't be found

A hope that your heart feels restored

A present helper in a time of trials and tribulations

Close to the Father of Hope and Grace

Long live King Jesus!

Yours to Lead

Jesus this life of mine
It is yours to lead
Though I may struggle
Though I may cry
Please never depart from me
Accept my heart as a letter to your promise
To always stay and to keep beside you
To allow you to lead me in any direction you choose
Because you are a good Father
Jesus, you are so good

He received

Jesus received him because he thinks of us all

He never leaves anyone behind

He is the shepherd of our souls

Searching for us and calling for us

Whenever he is ready

Jesus will come and rescue him

If he knocks

Jesus will always answer

Walking by Him

By walking by the Son of God

He can walk by the Father

Taste and see that the Lord is good

And his mercies endure forever

He was blessed and changed

Because Jesus Christ rose again

His life was the living testament

From being trapped in the inside

To be free to walk and live and roam by Jesus

Until it was time to come into the kingdom

Jesus Christ was the decorator inside

The hope that flushed out all the darkness

Until there was no more

Leadeth Me

He chose to let Jesus lead him

Because when he met Jesus, he could not see a path

The path before him was lonely and dark

Filled with memories of his past

Harsh shouts in his ear

But when Jesus Christ came

It changed again

He was healed and happy

Cleansed by the spirit

And brought up again

Changed so he could live

So, whenever Jesus walks

He will follow

Because in his darkest hours

The light is what kept him going

Alive by Him

He was alive through Jesus Christ
He who had saved and rescued him
A man who had died and rose again
He had time to rescue him
With nail-pierced hands
And a chance to breathe again
He told his disciples to change the world
For He had been changed
And so right now
The smallest man
Filled with a sense of darkness and loss of hope
Jesus Christ came to him
A touch of light
Took away all darkness

It will work out

No matter what you are going through
It will work out
Because anyone by Jesus's side
They will always be safe under his pavilion
No darkness or weapons can prosper
For when Jesus is there
The enemy and his minions will scatter
No matter what you are going through
Trust Jehovah Jireh!

Following Him

Following Jesus is so easy because

For the very first time in his life

He was free of all his issues

No longer would he have to spend years

Being in sin and shame

Finally, he was free to live again

With his second life

He would not make the same mistakes twice

Because Jesus Christ is by his side

Taste and See

"O taste and see that the LORD is good:

Blessed is the man that trusteth in him."

Psalm 34:8 KJV

The Lord Listens

He listened to him

The Lord listened to him

In his times of quarrel

When he argued with a person who just could not leave him

When he felt lost and alone

Jesus was there

The Lord listens to those who are struggling

And waits for their call

Once they call, he will surely answer

The Holy

The Lord is near

He is there and he cares

He loves and he hears

He is holy

Holy

Holy

The Lord is holy

And his mercies endure forever

Joy found in Him

His joy is found in Him

He is beside him

And he loves him

Joy and freedom are found in Jesus Christ

The Lord

The Lord is so good

The Lord is so merciful

He cares for him and everyone

Even the people who decided to turn their backs on him

His love is eternal

His works always worth in your favour

Changing and helping to give him thanks

The Lord is good and his mercies endure forever

Knowing

Knowing Jesus was a special thing
Which made him stronger than Him
Jesus is strong
Jesus is good
Jesus carried him through
And He helped him as a man, face the darkest days
Knowing Jesus is his special place
To be by his side
To learn and to grow
To love in a time of lost
To change oneself

Living God

Taking care of us

It is God's speciality

Loving and kindness are also qualities of his Kingdom

The living God listened to him

Helped him with his burdens

He was the light to his darkness

The living God sent down his love

And with that reassurance

He was able to be changed

From the love and the care of the true living God

Accepting Him

Accept Jesus Christ into your life

He restored and removed all the darkness

Offering you life itself

Through accepting him your heart and mind can be changed

The past can be forgotten

And strengthen through Jesus Christ can be found

Praise the Lord for he is good!

His mercies endure forever!

The Father is close to those who are heartbroken

He hears the cries of all his people

And he restores their soul

Praise the Lord, for he is good!

Giving light and turning away the darkness!

Praise Him!

Accept Him.

Printed in Great Britain
by Amazon

47381167R00067